Gluten-Free Korean Cookbook

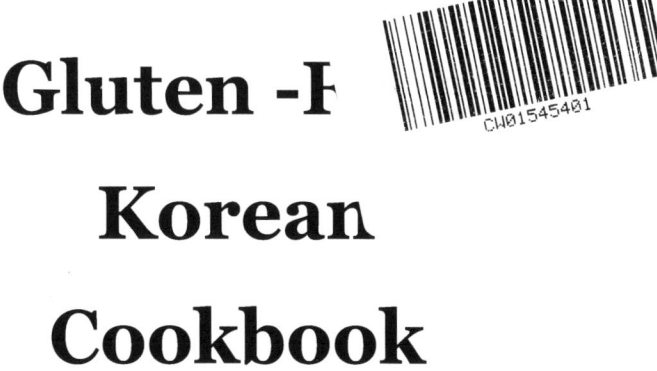

"Discover Delicious and Authentic Korean Recipes without the Gluten – with Over 60 Korean Gluten-free Recipes"

Keisha Wright

Disclaimer

The information contained in this nonfiction book is for general information purposes only. The author and publisher of this book have used their best efforts in preparing this book and the information provided herein.

In no event will the author or publisher be liable for any loss or damage including without limitation, indirect or consequential loss or damage, or any loss or damage whatsoever arising from loss of data or profits arising out of, or in connection with, the use of this book.

Copyright © 2022 by [Keisha wright]

All rights reserved. No part of this book may be reproduced in any form or by any electronic or mechanical means, including information storage and retrieval systems, without permission in writing from the publisher, except by a reviewer who may quote brief passages in a review.

Table of Content
CHAPTER 1: 11

Introduction to Gluten-Free 11

Korean Cooking 11

What is gluten and why is it important to avoid it?   12

   The basics of gluten-free cooking and ingredient substitutions 13

   An overview of Korean cooking techniques and ingredients 14

Chapter 2: **16**

Appetizers and Snacks 16

    Rice crackers 16

    (kkae-tteok) 16

    Spicy garlic green beans 17

    (namul) 17

    Spicy pickled radishes (kkakdugi) 17

    Fried chicken 19

    (dakgangjeong) 19

Chapter 3: **19**

Soups and Stews 21

    Beef bone broth 21

(seolleongtang) 21

Tofu and vegetable stew (sundubu jjigae) 22

Spicy seafood stew 23

(haemul pajeon) 23

Chapter 4: **24**

Rice and Noodles 24

Steamed white rice (bap) 24

Gluten-free soy sauce 25

(ganjang) 25

Cold noodles with spicy sauce (naengmyeon) 25

Stir-fried noodles 26

(japchae) 26

Chapter 5: **28**

Side Dishes and Pickles 28

Grilled eggplant 28

(gaji-namul) 28

Pickled daikon radish (danmuji) 29

Soybean Sprout Salad 29

(kongnamul-muchim) 29

Spicy pickled cucumbers 30

(oi-muchim) 30

Chapter 6: 31
Main Dishes 31
- Grilled bulgogi 31
- (neobiani) 31
- Spicy stir-fried chicken 33
- (Dakbokkeumtang) 33
- Braised beef short ribs 33
- (galbi-jjim) 33
- Grilled pork belly 34
- (samgyeopsal) 34
- Spicy pork and vegetables (jeyuk-bokkeum) 34
- Stir-fried squid 35
- (Ojingeo-bokkeum) 35

Chapter 7: 37
Soups and Stews 37
- Spicy kimchi stew 37
- (kimchi-jjigae) 37
- Soothing chicken soup 38
- (samgyetang) 38
- Beef and vegetable soup 39
- (seolleongtang) 39
- Spicy seafood stew 39

(Haemul-jjigae) 39
Gluten-free red bean ice cream 41
(Patbingsu) 41
Gluten-free rice cake balls 42
(Tteokbokki) 42
Korean barley tea 43
(boricha) 43

Chapter 8: 44
40-day gluten-free meal plan for a Korean cookbook 44

Chapter 9: 60
Gluten Free 60
Korean 60
Recipes 60
   Korean Rice Porridge (Juk) 60
   Grilled Korean BBQ Beef (Bulgogi) 62
   Korean Fried Chicken (Dakgangjeong) . 64
   Korean Spicy Tofu 66
   (Dubu Jorim) 66
   Korean Spicy Shrimp Stir Fry (Saewu Bokkeum) 68
   Korean Spicy Scallop Stir Fry (Jeonbok Bokkeum) 70

Korean Spicy Pork (Daeji Bulgogi) 73
Korean Spicy Squid Stir Fry (Ojingeo Bokkeum) 75
Korean Spicy Crab Stir Fry (Jangeo Bokkeum)...77
Korean Spicy Clam Stir Fry (Jogae Bokkeum) 79
Korean Spicy Chicken and Vegetable Stir Fry (Dak Bokkeum) 81
Korean Spicy 84
Beef and Vegetable Stir Fry 84
(Bulgogi Bokkeum) 84
Korean Multigrain Rice (Japgok-bap) with eggs and vegetables.......................86
Korean Fried Chicken (Dakgangjeong) with steamed rice and vegetables 89
Korean Rice Balls (Onigiri) filled with vegetables and pickled plum 92
Korean-style Pancakes (Jeons) filled with 94
vegetables and seafood 94
Korean Multigrain Rice (Japgokbap) with eggs and vegetables 97
Korean Soft Tofu Stew 99
(Soondubu Jjigae) 99

Korean Spicy Beef Soup (Yukgaejang). 102
Korean Seaweed Soup 104
(Miyeokguk) 104
Korean Chicken Soup (Dakgaejang) 106
Korean Mushroom Soup 108
(Beoseot Gomtang) 108
Korean Ox Tail Soup 109
(Kkorijjim) 109
Korean Pork Belly Soup (Samgyetang) 112
Korean Spicy Oyster Soup 114
(Gul Jjigae) 114
Korean Mushroom Soup 116
(Beoseot Gomtang) 116
Korean Seaweed Soup 118
(Miyeokguk) 118
Korean Beef and Radish Soup (Moo Saengchae) 119
Korean Sweet Rice Balls (Gyeongdan) .121
Korean Rice Cakes (Hwajeon) with sweet bean filling 123
Korean Steamed Egg 126
(Gyeran Jjim) 126

Korean Glutinous Rice Cake (Tteokbokki) 128
Sweet and Sour Chicken (Tongdak) 130
Korean Red Bean Porridge (Danpatjuk) 132

Chapter 10: **135**
Tips for adapting traditional 135
Korean recipes to be gluten-free 135
   Recommendations for 137
   Gluten-free Korean 137
   Ingredients and products 137

Chapter 11: **137**
Conclusion 140

CHAPTER 1:
Introduction to Gluten-Free Korean Cooking

Gluten, a protein present in wheat, barley, and rye, has sparked growing worry about its harmful health implications in recent years. Consuming gluten may cause a variety of digestive issues and other health concerns in those who have celiac disease or gluten sensitivity. As a result, in order to enhance their health and well-being, many individuals have resorted to gluten-free diets.

If you are gluten-free and like Korean food, you may be wondering how to modify traditional dishes to meet your dietary requirements. The good news is that many tasty and fulfilling Korean recipes can be easily gluten-free by making a few simple ingredient modifications.

In this chapter, we'll go over the fundamentals of gluten-free cooking as well as an introduction of Korean cooking methods and materials. You will have a solid basis for making tasty and authentic gluten-free Korean dishes by the conclusion of this chapter.

What is gluten and why is it important to avoid it?

Gluten is a protein present in wheat, barley, and rye that provides dough flexibility and aids in the rise of bread. It's also in a lot of processed meals, such sauces, soups, and processed meats, as well as non-food items like cosmetics and pharmaceuticals.

Consuming gluten may damage the lining of the gut and limit nutritional absorption in those who have celiac disease, an auto-immune illness that affects the small intestine. This may result in a variety of digestive disorders as well as other health concerns including anemia, osteoporosis, and nerve damage.

Gluten intolerance, also known as non-celiac gluten sensitivity, is a disorder in which patients feel symptoms similar to celiac disease after ingesting gluten but do not have the same inflammatory response or intestinal damage. The specific etiology of non-celiac gluten sensitivity is unknown, however it is thought to be connected to an immunological response or intolerance to particular gluten components.

The basics of gluten-free cooking and ingredient substitutions

If you are on a gluten-free diet, you must pay great attention to the ingredients in your food and exercise caution while dining out or buying pre-made items. Many processed meals and sauces include hidden sources of gluten, therefore it is important to read labels carefully and pick gluten-free items.

There are also several gluten-free alternatives to wheat-based items that may be used in recipes in lieu of wheat, barley, and rye. Rice flour, almond flour, and potato flour are examples of gluten-free flours. Gluten-free spaghetti and noodles made from rice, quinoa, or legumes are also popular.

When converting traditional Korean dishes to gluten-free, it is important to pay close attention to components such as soy sauce, which is usually manufactured from wheat, and to substitute gluten-free alternatives such as tamari or coconut aminos. Cross-contamination, which may occur when gluten-free meals come into touch with gluten-containing ingredients, utensils, or surfaces, should also be avoided.

An overview of Korean cooking techniques and ingredients

Korean cuisine is renowned for its robust tastes and diverse menu offerings, which include anything from fiery stews and soups to grilled meats and pickled veggies. Many

Korean recipes revolve on rice and a variety of banchan, or tiny plates of pickled or seasoned vegetables, tofu, or fish.

Grilling, frying, and stir-frying are common Korean culinary methods, as are fermentation and pickling.

Chapter 2:
Appetizers and Snacks

Appetizers and snacks, known as "banchan" in Korean cuisine, are an essential component of the dinner. These little plates of pickled or sea-salted veggies, tofu, or shellfish are designed to be shared with rice and main courses. Many banchan may be easily gluten-free by making a few simple ingredient substitutions.

To try, here are some tasty and filling gluten-free Korean appetizers and snacks:

Rice crackers (kkae-tteok)

Kkae-tteok are crispy, flavorful rice crackers that are often served as an appetizer or snack. Cooked short-grain rice is combined with a variety of spices and formed into little balls or discs. After that, the crackers are deep-fried till golden and crispy.

To make kkae-tteok gluten-free, use gluten-free soy sauce or tamari for ordinary soy sauce and cook in gluten-free oil. To give the crackers more taste, you may add a number of gluten-free spices such as sesame seeds, seaweed flakes, or chili flakes.

Spicy garlic green beans (namul)

Namul is a seasoned vegetable dish that is often served as a banchan. One popular variation uses thin strips of blanched green beans mixed in a spicy garlic sauce.

To create gluten-free spicy garlic green beans, prepare the sauce using gluten-free soy sauce or tamari and cook with gluten-free oil. To give the meal more flavor, you may add gluten-free spices such sesame seeds, gochugaru (Korean chili flakes), and scallions.

Spicy pickled radishes (kkakdugi)

Kkakdugi is a traditional Korean banchan composed of diced radishes pickled in a spicy combination of gochugaru, vinegar, and sugar. The radishes are crisp and somewhat sweet, with a kick from the chili flakes.

To prepare gluten-free kkakdugi, use gluten-free vinegar and gluten-free soy sauce or tamari in the pickling mixture. You may also add a variety of additional ingredients, such as garlic, ginger, and scallions, to enhance the taste of the meal.

Fried chicken (dakgangjeong)

Dakgangjeong is a famous Korean snack or appetizer comprised of bite-sized fried chicken covered in a sweet and spicy sauce. The chicken is often coated in a flour and spice combination before being deep-fried till golden and crispy.

To create gluten-free dakgangjeong, cover the chicken in a gluten-free flour or breadcrumb mixture and cook in gluten-free oil. To add flavor to the meal, use gluten-free soy sauce or tamari in the sauce.

In addition to these appetizers and snacks, the world of Korean cuisine offers a plethora of additional delectable and fulfilling gluten-free alternatives. There is something for everyone, from flavorful soups and stews to rice and noodle meals. In the next chapters, we will go through some of these foods in more depth, including recipes and recommendations for making them gluten-free.

As you begin your gluten-free Korean culinary adventure, keep in mind that experimenting with new ingredients and methods is half of the joy. Don't be afraid to experiment and modify recipes to fit your taste preferences and nutritional requirements. With a little imagination and help from this cookbook, you'll be well on your way to making tasty and genuine gluten-free Korean dishes that will wow.

Chapter 3:
Soups and Stews

Soups and stews are staples of Korean cuisine, and there are many tasty and filling alternatives that are inherently gluten-free or can be simply altered to be gluten-free with a few easy ingredient swaps. These meals, ranging from substantial beef bone broth to spicy seafood stew, are ideal for warming up on a chilly day or gratifying a taste for robust flavors.

To try, here are some tasty and filling gluten-free Korean soups and stews:

Beef bone broth (Seolleongtang)

Seolleongtang is a milky white beef bone broth that is often served with thin slices of beef and green onions. It is made by simmering beef bones and marrow for several hours until the broth is rich and flavorful.

To make gluten-free seolleongtang, be sure to use a gluten-free beef broth and a gluten-free soy sauce or tamari in the seasoning mixture. You can also add a variety of other ingredients, such as garlic, ginger, and scallions, to give the broth extra flavor.

Tofu and vegetable stew (sundubu jjigae)

Sundubu jjigae is a spicy tofu and vegetable stew that is often eaten with rice. Soft tofu, veggies, and a spicy broth prepared with gochugaru and seafood or anchovy stock are used to make this dish.

To prepare gluten-free sundubu jjigae, cook the stew using gluten-free broth and gluten-free soy sauce or tamari. You may also add a variety of additional gluten-free items, such as vegetables, tofu, and seafood, to add taste and nutrition to the stew.

Spicy seafood stew (haemul pajeon)

Haemul pajeon is a spicy seafood and green onion pancake eaten as a stew. It is prepared with a variety of shellfish (clams, mussels, and squid) and green onions that are coated in flour and eggs then pan-fried till crispy.

To create gluten-free haemul pajeon, cover the fish and veggies in a gluten-free flour or breadcrumb mixture and cook in gluten-free oil. To add flavor to the meal, use gluten-free soy sauce or tamari in the dipping sauce.

Chapter 4:
Rice and Noodles

Rice and noodles are classics in Korean cuisine, and there are many tasty and filling recipes that are inherently gluten-free or can be readily altered with a few easy ingredient replacements. These foods are ideal for every occasion, from steaming white rice to cold noodles with spicy sauce.

To explore, here are some tasty and filling gluten-free Korean rice and noodle dishes:

Steamed white rice (bap)

Many Korean dishes are built on steamed white rice, known as bap in Korean. It's easy to prepare and only takes three ingredients: short-grain white rice, water, and a sprinkle of salt.

To prepare gluten-free bap, use a gluten-free brand of short-grain white rice and cook according to the package directions. Other ingredients, such as sesame seeds or seaweed flakes, may be added to enhance the taste of the rice.

Gluten-free soy sauce (Ganjang)

Ganjang is a sort of soy sauce used in Korean cuisine. It has a deep and savory taste and is prepared by fermenting soybeans, wheat, and water.

In order to prepare gluten-free ganjang, use gluten-free soy sauce. Many brands are available that are manufactured only of soybeans and water, with no wheat added. As a gluten-free substitute to ganjang, you may use different sauces like as tamari or coconut aminos.

Cold noodles with spicy sauce (naengmyeon)

Naengmyeon is a famous Korean meal that consists of thin, chewy noodles cooked from potato, sweet potato, or buckwheat starch. The noodles are often served cold, with a spicy sauce comprised of gochujang, mustard, and vinegar.

Use gluten-free noodles produced from potato, sweet potato, or buckwheat starch to prepare gluten-free naengmyeon. In the sauce, use gluten-free gochujang and gluten-free soy sauce or tamari. You may also add a number of additional ingredients, such as boiled egg, pear, and meat, to add taste and nutrients to the meal.

Stir-fried noodles (Japchae)

Japchae is a famous Korean noodle dish comprised of sweet potato noodles stir-fried with veggies and meat. Soy sauce, sugar, and sesame oil are often used to season the noodles.

To prepare gluten-free Japchae, use a gluten-free soy sauce or tamari with the spice mixture and fry using a gluten-free oil. You may also add gluten-free foods like veggies, meat, and eggs to give the meal more taste and nutrients.

Chapter 5:
Side Dishes and Pickles

Side dishes, or "banchan," are an essential component of Korean cuisine and are supposed to be shared. Many side dishes and pickles are naturally gluten-free or can be easily adapted to be gluten-free with a few simple ingredient substitutions. These dishes, ranging from grilled eggplant to pickled daikon radish, are ideal for adding flavor and nutrition to any meal.

Here are some delicious gluten-free Korean side dishes and pickles to try:

Grilled eggplant (Gaji-namul)

Gaji-namul is a spicy vegetable dish prepared from grilled or pan-fried eggplant. It's usually seasoned with a combination of soy sauce, garlic, and sesame oil.

To prepare gluten-free gaji-namul, use a gluten-free soy sauce or tamari with the spice mixture and cook using a gluten-free oil. You may also add gluten-free ingredients like garlic, scallions, and sesame seeds to give the meal more flavor.

Pickled daikon radish (danmuji)

Danmuji is a famous Korean banchan prepared from thinly sliced daikon radish pickled in a vinegar, sugar, and salt combination. The radish is crisp and sweet, with a tart note from the vinegar.

Use gluten-free vinegar in the pickling mixture to produce gluten-free danmuji. Other ingredients, such as garlic, ginger, and scallions, may be added to enhance the taste of the pickle.

Soybean Sprout Salad (Kongnamul-muchim)

Kongnamul-muchim is a seasoned vegetable dish prepared with boiling soybean sprouts and a variety of ingredients such garlic, onions, and sesame seeds. It's often served as a side dish or as a garnish for rice and noodles.

To prepare gluten-free kongnamul-muchim, use a gluten-free soy sauce or tamari with the seasoning combination and cook using a gluten-free oil. You may also add gluten-free foods like vegetables, tofu, and fish to give the meal more taste and nutrients.

Spicy pickled cucumbers (Oi-muchim)

Oi-muchim is a famous Korean banchan prepared with thinly sliced cucumbers pickled in a blend of gochugaru, vine-gar, and sugar. Cucumbers are crisp and sweet, with a touch of spice from the chili flakes.

Use gluten-free vinegar and soy sauce or tamari in the pickling mixture to produce gluten-free oi-muchim. Other ingredients, such as garlic, ginger, and scallions, may be added to enhance the taste of the pickle.

Chapter 6:
Main Dishes

Main meals in Korean cuisine are usually based on a protein, such as beef, chicken, or pig, and are served with rice, vegetables, and a variety of side dishes. Many Korean major meals are inherently gluten-free or may be readily gluten-free by making a few easy ingredient substitutions. These recipes are ideal for every occasion, from grilled Bulgogi to spicy stir-fried chicken.

Here are some tasty gluten-free Korean main meals to try:

Grilled Bulgogi (Neobiani)

Bulgogi is a famous Korean meal prepared with grilled or pan-fried thin slices of marinated beef. Traditionally, the beef is marinated in a blend of soy sauce, sugar, and different seasonings such as garlic and scallions.

To create gluten-free Bulgogi, use gluten-free soy sauce or tamari in the marinade and gluten-free frying oil. You may also add gluten-free foods like vegetables, tofu, and fish to give the meal more taste and nutrients.

Spicy stir-fried chicken (Dakbokkeumtang)

Dakbokkeumtang is a spicy stir-fried chicken dish that is often served with rice and a variety of side dishes. Typically, the chicken is coated in flour and spices before being stir-fried with a spicy sauce prepared with gochujang and assorted veggies.

To create gluten-free dakbokkeumtang, cover the chicken with a gluten-free flour or breadcrumb mixture and fry using a gluten-free oil. To add more flavor to the meal, use gluten-free gochujang and gluten-free soy sauce or tamari in the sauce.

Braised beef short ribs (Galbi-jjim)

Galbi-jjim is a rich and savory braised beef meal that is often served with rice and a variety of side dishes. Before braising in a delicious broth, the beef is often marinated in a blend of soy sauce, sugar, and different spices.

Use gluten-free soy sauce or tamari in the marinade and gluten-free broth for braising to produce gluten-free galbi-jjim. You may also add gluten-free foods like veggies and tofu to give the meal more taste and nutrients.

Grilled pork belly (Samgyeopsal)

Samgyeopsal is a famous Korean cuisine that consists of thick slices of grilled pig belly served with a variety of side dishes and dipping sauces. Before grilling or pan-frying, the pork is often marinated in a combination of soy sauce, sugar, and other spices.

To create gluten-free samgyeopsal, use gluten-free soy sauce or tamari in the marinade and gluten-free cooking oil. You may also add a range of additional gluten-free items, such as veggies, tofu, and fish, to add taste and nutrition to the recipe.

Spicy pork and vegetables (jeyuk-bokkeum)

Jeyuk-bokkeum is a popular spicy stir-fried pork and vegetable dish in Korean cuisine. It's created with thin slices of pork stir-fried with veggies and a spicy sauce made with gochujang and other ingredients.

To create gluten-free jeyuk-bokkeum, make the sauce using gluten-free gochujang and gluten-

free soy sauce or tamari, and cook with gluten-free oil. You may also add gluten-free foods like vegetables, tofu, and fish to give the meal more taste and nutrients.

Stir-fried squid (Ojingeo-bokkeum)

Ojingeo-bokkeum is a renowned spicy stir-fried squid dish in Korean cuisine. It's created with thinly sliced squid stir-fried with veggies and a spicy sauce made with gochujang and other ingredients.

To create gluten-free Ojingeo-bokkeum, make the sauce using gluten-free gochujang and gluten-free soy sauce or tamari, and cook with gluten-free oil. You may also add gluten-free foods like vegetables, tofu, and fish to give the meal more taste and nutrients.

Ojingeo-bokkeum is a tasty and filling main meal suitable for any occasion. It is often served with rice and a selection of side dishes such as pickled cucumbers, seasoned bean sprouts, and kimchi. It may also be eaten as a side dish with rice and noodles, or wrapped in

lettuce or perilla leaves for a light and filling supper.

Chapter 7:
Soups and Stews

Soups and stews are an important aspect of Korean cuisine and are often served as a main dish or as a side dish to be shared. Many soups and stews are inherently gluten-free or may be readily gluten-free by making a few easy ingredient modifications. These meals, ranging from hot kimchi stew to relaxing chicken soup, are ideal for adding flavor and nutrition to any meal.

To try, here are some tasty and filling gluten-free Korean soups and stews:

Spicy kimchi stew (Kimchi-jjigae)

Kimchi-jjigae is a traditional Korean stew cooked with fermented kimchi, tofu, and other veggies. It has a spicy and savory taste and is often seasoned with a blend of gochugaru, soy sauce, and different seasonings.

To prepare gluten-free kimchi-jjigae, combine gluten-free gochugaru, gluten-free soy sauce or tamari, and gluten-free tofu in the spice combination. To add taste and nutrition to the stew, you may add a range of gluten-free items such as vegetables, fish, and meat.

Soothing chicken soup (Samgyetang)

Samgyetang is a traditional Korean soup cooked with a whole young chicken filled with glutinous rice, ginseng, and a variety of herbs before simmering in a flavorful broth. The soup is often served as a main course and is said to have both nutritional and therapeutic effects.

To create gluten-free Samgyetang, start with gluten-free rice and finish with gluten-free broth. You may also add gluten-free foods like vegetables, herbs, and spices to give the soup more taste and nutrients.

Beef and vegetable soup (Seolleongtang)

The traditional Korean soup seolleongtang is prepared with slow-cooked beef and a variety of veggies. It has a deep and savory taste and is often seasoned with a blend of salt and pepper.

To create gluten-free seolleongtang, simmer the beef and veggies in a gluten-free broth. You may also add additional gluten-free items, such as herbs and spices, to add flavor and nutrients to the soup.

Spicy seafood stew (Haemul-jjigae)

Haemul-jjigae is a hot Korean stew cooked with seafood and a spicy sauce made with gochujang and other ingredients. It is often served with a bowl of rice and a selection of side dishes.

To create gluten-free haemul-jjigae, make the sauce using gluten-free gochujang and gluten-free soy sauce or tamari, and boil the shellfish in gluten-free broth. You may also add gluten-free foods like veggies and tofu to give the stew more flavor and nutrients.

In addition to these soups and stews, the world of Korean cuisine offers a plethora of other delectable and fulfilling gluten-free alternatives. There is something for everyone, from main courses and side dishes to desserts and beverages. In the next chapters, we'll go through some of these foods in more depth, as well as give recipes and recommendations for making them gluten-free.

Gluten-free red bean ice cream (Patbingsu)

Patbingsu is a famous Korean delicacy that consists of shaved ice with a variety of delicious toppings such as red bean paste, fruit, and ice cream. It is a refreshing and pleasant delicacy that is often offered throughout the summer months.

Use gluten-free ice cream and gluten-free red bean paste to create gluten-free patbingsu. You may also top the pie with gluten-free toppings like fruit, almonds, and chocolate to add taste and nutrition.

Patbingsu is a delectable and filling dessert that is suitable for any occasion. It is often served in a big bowl and is intended to be shared. It's delicious on its own or as a garnish for rice cakes or pancakes.

Gluten-free rice cake balls (Tteokbokki)

Tteokbokki is a famous Korean street meal that consists of soft rice cakes topped with a spicy sauce prepared with gochujang and other ingredients. It is often served as a snack or as a side dish with rice and noodles.

To prepare gluten-free tteokbokki, create the sauce using gluten-free gochujang and gluten-free soy sauce or tamari, and use gluten-free rice cake. You may also add gluten-free foods like vegetables, tofu, and fish to give the meal more taste and nutrients.

Tteokbokki is a tasty and filling snack that is suitable for any occasion. It is often served in a big bowl and is intended to be shared. It may be eaten on its own or as a side dish with rice or noodles.

Korean barley tea (Boricha)

Boricha is a famous Korean tea that is created by steeping roasted barley grains in hot water. It is a pleasant and calming beverage that is often offered as an addition to a meal or as a solo beverage.

When making gluten-free Boricha, use gluten-free barley and gluten-free water for steeping. Other ingredients, including as honey, lemon, and ginger, may be added to the tea to provide taste and nutrients.

Boricha is a tasty and pleasant drink that is appropriate for any occasion. It is often served in a big teapot and is intended to be shared. Depending on your desire, it may be served hot or cold.

Chapter 8:

40-day gluten-free meal plan for a Korean cookbook

Day 1:

Breakfast: Korean Rice Porridge (Juk) with eggs and vegetables

Lunch: Grilled Korean BBQ Beef (Bulgogi) with steamed rice and vegetables

Dinner: Korean Spicy Tofu (Dubu Jorim) with steamed rice and vegetables

Day 2:

Breakfast: Korean-style Omelette (Gyeran Mari) with vegetables

Lunch: Korean Spicy Pork (Daeji Bulgogi) with steamed rice and vegetables

Dinner: Korean Fried Chicken (Dakgangjeong) with steamed rice and vegetables

Day 3:

Breakfast: Korean Multigrain Rice (Japgokbap) with eggs and vegetables

Lunch: Korean Beef and Vegetable Stir Fry (Yakiniku) with steamed rice and vegetables

Dinner: Korean Spicy Chicken Stir Fry (Dak Bokkeum) with steamed rice and vegetables

Day 4:

Breakfast: Korean Rice Balls (Onigiri) filled with vegetables and pickled plum

Lunch: Korean Spicy Tofu (Dubu Jorim) with steamed rice and vegetables

Dinner: Korean Spicy Shrimp Stir Fry (Saewu Bokkeum) with steamed rice and vegetables

Day 5:

Breakfast: Korean-style Pancakes (Jeon) filled with vegetables and seafood

Lunch: Grilled Korean BBQ Beef (Bulgogi) with steamed rice and vegetables

Dinner: Korean Spicy Scallop Stir Fry (Jeonbok Bokkeum) with steamed rice and vegetables

Day 6:

Breakfast: Korean Rice Porridge (Juk) with eggs and vegetables

Lunch: Korean Spicy Pork (Daeji Bulgogi) with steamed rice and vegetables

Dinner: Korean Beef and Vegetable Stir Fry (Yakiniku) with steamed rice and vegetables

Day 7:

Breakfast: Korean Multigrain Rice (Japgokbap) with eggs and vegetables

Lunch: Korean Fried Chicken (Dakgangjeong) with steamed rice and vegetables

Dinner: Korean Spicy Chicken Stir Fry (Dak Bokkeum) with steamed rice and vegetables

Day 8:

Breakfast: Korean Rice Balls (Onigiri) filled with vegetables and pickled plum

Lunch: Korean Spicy Tofu (Dubu Jorim) with steamed rice and vegetables

Dinner: Korean Spicy Shrimp Stir Fry (Saewu Bokkeum) with steamed rice and vegetables

Day 9:

Breakfast: Korean-style Pancakes (Jeons) filled with vegetables and seafood

Lunch: Grilled Korean BBQ Beef (Bulgogi) with steamed rice and vegetables

Dinner: Korean Spicy Scallop Stir Fry (Jeonbok Bokkeum) with steamed rice and vegetables

Day 10:

Breakfast: Korean Rice Porridge (Juk) with eggs and vegetables

Lunch: Korean Spicy Pork (Daeji Bulgogi) with steamed rice and vegetables

Dinner: Korean Beef and Vegetable Stir Fry (Yakiniku) with steamed rice and vegetables

Day 11:

Breakfast: Korean Multigrain Rice (Japgokbap) with eggs and vegetables

Lunch: Korean Fried Chicken (Dakgangjeong) with steamed rice and vegetables

Dinner: Korean Spicy Chicken Stir Fry (Dak Bokkeum) with steamed rice and vegetables

Day 12:

Breakfast: Korean Rice Balls (Onigiri) filled with vegetables and pickled plum

Lunch: Korean Spicy Tofu (Dubu Jorim) with steamed rice and vegetables

Dinner: Korean Spicy Shrimp Stir Fry (Saewu Bokkeum) with steamed rice and vegetables

Day 13:

Breakfast: Korean-style Pancakes (Jeons) filled with vegetables and seafood

Lunch: Grilled Korean BBQ Beef (Bulgogi) with steamed rice and vegetables

Dinner: Korean Spicy Scallop Stir Fry (Jeonbok Bokkeum) with steamed rice and vegetables

Day 14:

Breakfast: Korean Rice Porridge (Juk) with eggs and vegetables

Lunch: Korean Spicy Pork (Daeji Bulgogi) with steamed rice and vegetables

Dinner: Korean Beef and Vegetable Stir Fry (Yakiniku) with steamed rice and vegetables

Day 15:

Breakfast: Korean Multigrain Rice (Japgokbap) with eggs and vegetables

Lunch: Korean Fried Chicken (Dakgangjeong) with steamed rice and vegetables

Dinner: Korean Spicy Chicken Stir Fry (Dak Bokkeum) with steamed rice and vegetables

Day 16:

Breakfast: Korean Rice Balls (Onigiri) filled with vegetables and pickled plum

Lunch: Korean Spicy Tofu (Dubu Jorim) with steamed rice and vegetables

Dinner: Korean Spicy Shrimp Stir Fry (Saewu Bokkeum) with steamed rice and vegetables

Day 17:

Breakfast: Korean-style Pancakes (Jeons) filled with vegetables and seafood

Lunch: Grilled Korean BBQ Beef (Bulgogi) with steamed rice and vegetables

Dinner: Korean Spicy Scallop Stir Fry (Jeonbok Bokkeum) with steamed rice and vegetables

Day 18:

Breakfast: Korean Rice Porridge (Juk) with eggs and vegetables

Lunch: Korean Spicy Pork (Daeji Bulgogi) with steamed rice and vegetables

Dinner: Korean Beef and Vegetable Stir Fry (Yakiniku) with steamed rice and vegetables

Day 19:

Breakfast: Korean Multigrain Rice (Japgokbap) with eggs and vegetables

Lunch: Korean Fried Chicken (Dakgangjeong) with steamed rice and vegetables

Dinner: Korean Spicy Chicken Stir Fry (Dak Bokkeum) with steamed rice and vegetables

Day 20:

Breakfast: Korean Rice Balls (Onigiri) filled with vegetables and pickled plum

Lunch: Korean Spicy Tofu (Dubu Jorim) with steamed rice and vegetables

Dinner: Korean Spicy Shrimp Stir Fry (Saewu Bokkeum) with steamed rice and vegetables

Day 21:

Breakfast: Korean-style Pancakes (Jeons) filled with vegetables and seafood

Lunch: Grilled Korean BBQ Beef (Bulgogi) with steamed rice and vegetables

Dinner: Korean Spicy Scallop Stir Fry (Jeonbok Bokkeum) with steamed rice and vegetables

Day 22:

Breakfast: Korean Rice Porridge (Juk) with eggs and vegetables

Lunch: Korean Spicy Pork (Daeji Bulgogi) with steamed rice and vegetables

Dinner: Korean Beef and Vegetable Stir Fry (Yakiniku) with steamed rice and vegetables

Day 23:

Breakfast: Korean Multigrain Rice (Japgokbap) with eggs and vegetables

Lunch: Korean Fried Chicken (Dakgangjeong) with steamed rice and vegetables

Dinner: Korean Spicy Chicken Stir Fry (Dak Bokkeum) with steamed rice and vegetables

Breakfast: Korean Rice Balls (Onigiri) filled with vegetables and pickled plum

Lunch: Korean Spicy Tofu (Dubu Jorim) with steamed rice and vegetables

Dinner: Korean Spicy Shrimp Stir Fry (Saewu Bokkeum) with steamed rice and vegetables

Day 25:

Breakfast: Korean-style Pancakes (Jeons) filled with vegetables and seafood

Lunch: Grilled Korean BBQ Beef (Bulgogi) with steamed rice and vegetables

Dinner: Korean Spicy Scallop Stir Fry (Jeonbok Bokkeum) with steamed rice and vegetables

Day 26:

Breakfast: Korean Rice Porridge (Juk) with eggs and vegetables

Lunch: Korean Spicy Pork (Daeji Bulgogi) with steamed rice and vegetables

Dinner: Korean Beef and Vegetable Stir Fry (Yakiniku) with steamed rice and vegetables

Day 27:

Breakfast: Korean Multigrain Rice (Japgokbap) with eggs and vegetables

Lunch: Korean Fried Chicken (Dakgangjeong) with steamed rice and vegetables

Dinner: Korean Spicy Chicken Stir Fry (Dak Bokkeum) with steamed rice and vegetables

Day 28:

Breakfast: Korean Rice Balls (Onigiri) filled with vegetables and pickled plum

Lunch: Korean Spicy Tofu (Dubu Jorim) with steamed rice and vegetables

Dinner: Korean Spicy Shrimp Stir Fry (Saewu Bokkeum) with steamed rice and vegetables

Day 29:

Breakfast: Korean-style Pancakes (Jeons) filled with vegetables and seafood

Lunch: Grilled Korean BBQ Beef (Bulgogi) with steamed rice and vegetables

Dinner: Korean Spicy Scallop Stir Fry (Jeonbok Bokkeum) with steamed rice and vegetables

Day 30:

Breakfast: Korean Rice Porridge (Juk) with eggs and vegetables

Lunch: Korean Spicy Pork (Daeji Bulgogi) with steamed rice and vegetables

Dinner: Korean Beef and Vegetable Stir Fry (Yakiniku) with steamed rice and vegetables

Day 31:

Breakfast: Korean Multigrain Rice (Japgokbap) with eggs and vegetables

Lunch: Korean Fried Chicken (Dakgangjeong) with steamed rice and vegetables

Dinner: Korean Spicy Chicken Stir Fry (Dak Bokkeum) with steamed rice and vegetables

Day 32:

Breakfast: Korean Rice Balls (Onigiri) filled with vegetables and pickled plum

Lunch: Korean Spicy Tofu (Dubu Jorim) with steamed rice and vegetables

Dinner: Korean Spicy Shrimp Stir Fry (Saewu Bokkeum) with steamed rice and vegetables

Day 33:

Breakfast: Korean-style Pancakes (Jeons) filled with vegetables and seafood

Lunch: Grilled Korean BBQ Beef (Bulgogi) with steamed rice and vegetables

Dinner: Korean Spicy Scallop Stir Fry (Jeonbok Bokkeum) with steamed rice and vegetables

Day 34:

Breakfast: Korean Rice Porridge (Juk) with eggs and vegetables

Lunch: Korean Spicy Pork (Daeji Bulgogi) with steamed rice and vegetables

Dinner: Korean Beef and Vegetable Stir Fry (Yakiniku) with steamed rice and vegetables

Day 35:

Breakfast: Korean Multigrain Rice (Japgokbap) with eggs and vegetables

Lunch: Korean Fried Chicken (Dakgangjeong) with steamed rice and vegetables

Dinner: Korean Spicy Chicken Stir Fry (Dak Bokkeum) with steamed rice and vegetables

Day 36:

Breakfast: Korean Rice Balls (Onigiri) filled with vegetables and pickled plum

Lunch: Korean Spicy Tofu (Dubu Jorim) with steamed rice and vegetables

Dinner: Korean Spicy Shrimp Stir Fry (Saewu Bokkeum) with steamed rice and vegetables

Day 37:

Breakfast: Korean-style Pancakes (Jeons) filled with vegetables and seafood

Lunch: Grilled Korean BBQ Beef (Bulgogi) with steamed rice and vegetables

Dinner: Korean Spicy Scallop Stir Fry (Jeonbok Bokkeum) with steamed rice and vegetables

Day 38:

Breakfast: Korean Rice Porridge (Juk) with eggs and vegetables

Lunch: Korean Spicy Pork (Daeji Bulgogi) with steamed rice and vegetables

Dinner: Korean Beef and Vegetable Stir Fry (Yakiniku) with steamed rice and vegetables

Day 39:

Breakfast: Korean Multigrain Rice (Japgokbap) with eggs and vegetables

Lunch: Korean Fried Chicken (Dakgangjeong) with steamed rice and vegetables

Dinner: Korean Spicy Chicken Stir Fry (Dak Bokkeum) with steamed rice and vegetables

Day 40:

Breakfast: Korean Rice Balls (Onigiri) filled with vegetables and pickled plum

Lunch: Korean Spicy Tofu (Dubu Jorim) with steamed rice and vegetables

Dinner: Korean Spicy Shrimp Stir Fry (Saewu Bokkeum) with steamed rice and vegetables

Chapter 9:
Gluten Free Korean Recipes
Korean Rice Porridge (Juk)

This rice porridge, also known as "juk," is a traditional breakfast meal in Korea prepared with rice, water, and a variety of items including veggies, eggs, and meats. It is a filling and healthy dish that is simple to prepare and liked by people of all ages.

Total Time: 40 minutes

Servings: 4

Ingredients:

1 cup short grain rice

4 cups water

1 cup mixed vegetables (such as carrots, zucchini, and peas)

2 eggs

1 green onion, chopped

Salt, to taste

Directions:

• Rinse the rice until the water runs clear, then combine it with 4 cups of water in a saucepan. Bring the water to a boil, then reduce to a low heat and continue to cook for 30 minutes, or until the rice is tender and has absorbed all of the water.

• In the meanwhile, cut the veggies into tiny pieces and put them aside. In a separate dish, whisk together the eggs and put aside.

• When the rice is done, add the veggies and continue to cook for 5-10 minutes, or until the vegetables are soft.

• Pour in the beaten eggs and gently whisk to incorporate.

• Cook for another 2-3 minutes, or until the eggs are completely cooked.

Before serving, season with salt to taste and top with chopped green onion.

Nutritional Information (per serving):

Calories: 204

Protein: 8g

Fat: 3g

Carbohydrates: 41g

Fiber: 2g

Sodium: 44mg

Grilled Korean BBQ Beef (Bulgogi)

Bulgogi, also known as grilled Korean BBQ meat, is a popular Korean cuisine prepared from thin slices of marinated beef that are grilled or pan-fried to perfection. It's delicious, salty, and somewhat sweet, and it works nicely with steaming rice and veggies.

Total Time: 30 minutes

Servings: 4

Ingredients:

1 lb thinly sliced beef (such as sirloin or ribeye)

1/4 cup soy sauce

2 tbsp brown sugar

1 tbsp sesame oil

2 cloves garlic, minced

1 green onion, finely chopped

1/2 tsp black pepper

1/2 tsp sesame seeds

Directions:

• Combine the soy sauce, brown sugar, sesame oil, minced garlic, and chopped green onion, black pepper, and sesame seeds in a small bowl.

• To create the marinade, combine all of the ingredients in a mixing bowl.

• Pour the marinade over the beef pieces in a large mixing basin. Massage the marinade into the meat slices with your hands, ensuring that they are uniformly coated.

• Refrigerate the beef for at least 30 minutes, or up to 8 hours, after wrapping it in plastic wrap.

• Preheat a grill or a big skillet on high.

• Grill or pan-fry the beef slices in batches, being careful not to overcrowd the pan, for 2-3 minutes each side, or until done to your liking.

• Serve the grilled beef over steaming rice and a salad of lettuce, carrots, cucumbers, and onions.

Nutritional Information (per serving):

Calories: 216

Protein: 24g

Fat: 10g

Carbohydrates: 13g

Fiber: 0g

Sodium: 865mg

Korean Fried Chicken (Dakgangjeong)

Dakgangjeong, also known as Korean fried chicken, is a famous Korean snack comprised of marinated chicken pieces covered in a crispy and crunchy batter and deep-fried to perfection. It's spicy, sweet, and flavorful, and it combines nicely with steaming rice and a variety of vegetable side dishes.

Total Time: 1 hour

Servings: 4

Ingredients:

1 lb boneless, skinless chicken breasts or thighs

1 cup cornstarch

1 cup water

1 tbsp gochujang (Korean red pepper paste)

1 tbsp soy sauce

1 tbsp honey

1 tsp garlic powder

1 tsp onion powder

Vegetable oil, for frying

Directions:

- Set aside the chicken in little bite-sized pieces.

- To prepare the batter, combine the cornstarch and water in a small basin. Dip the chicken pieces into the batter, coating them evenly.

- To prepare the sauce, combine the gochujang, soy sauce, honey, garlic powder, and onion powder in a separate small bowl.

- Heat enough vegetable oil in a big saucepan or deep fryer to completely immerse the chicken pieces.

- When the oil is heated, gently add the coated chicken pieces to the pot or fryer and cook for 5-7 minutes, or until the chicken is done and the batter is crispy and golden brown.

- Remove the fried chicken from the oil and place it on a paper towel to drain. Toss the chicken in the sauce until well covered.

- Serve the fried chicken with steamed rice and a salad of lettuce, carrots, cucumbers, and onions.

Nutritional Information (per serving):

Calories: 430

Protein: 32g

Fat: 18g

Carbohydrates: 37g

Fiber: 1g

Sodium: 672mg

Korean Spicy Tofu (Dubu Jorim)

Dubu jorim, often known as spicy tofu, is a popular Korean side dish prepared from tofu cooked in a spicy and delicious sauce. It's simple to prepare, healthful, and delicious with steamed rice and a choice of veggies.

Total Time: 30 minutes

Servings: 4

Ingredients:

1 lb firm tofu, drained and cut into small cubes

2 tbsp vegetable oil

2 cloves garlic, minced

1 tsp gochujang (Korean red pepper paste)

1 tsp soy sauce

1 tsp sugar

1/2 cup water

1 green onion, finely chopped

Sesame seeds, for garnish

Directions:

- In a large saucepan over medium heat, heat the vegetable oil. Stir in the minced garlic for 30 seconds, or until fragrant.

- Stir-fry the tofu cubes in the pan for 2-3 minutes, or until gently browned.

- Combine the gochujang, soy sauce, sugar, and water in a mixing bowl. Bring the mixture to a boil, then lower to a low heat and continue to cook for 10-15 minutes, or until the sauce has thickened and the tofu has finished cooking.

- Before serving, garnish the spicy tofu with chopped green onions and sesame seeds.

- Serve the spicy tofu over steamed rice and a salad of lettuce, carrots, cucumbers, and onions.

Nutritional Information (per serving):

Calories: 152

Protein: 10g

Fat: 10g

Carbohydrates: 9g

Fiber: 3g

Sodium: 274mg

Korean Spicy Shrimp Stir Fry (Saewu Bokkeum)

Saewu bokkeum, also known as spicy shrimp stir fry, is a famous Korean cuisine that consists of stir-fried shrimp and veggies in a spicy and flavorful sauce. It's simple to prepare, tasty, and pairs great with steamed rice and a variety of vegetables.

Total Time: 30 minutes

Servings: 4

Ingredients:

1 lb large shrimp, peeled and deveined

2 tbsp vegetable oil

2 cloves garlic, minced

1 tsp gochujang (Korean red pepper paste)

1 tsp soy sauce

1 tsp sugar

1/2 cup water

1 green onion, finely chopped

Sesame seeds, for garnish

Directions:

- In a large saucepan over medium heat, heat the vegetable oil. Stir in the minced garlic for 30 seconds, or until fragrant.

- Stir-fry the shrimp for 2-3 minutes, or until they are pink and cooked through.

- Combine the gochujang, soy sauce, sugar, and water in a mixing bowl. Bring the mixture to a boil, then lower to a low heat and continue to cook for 5-7 minutes, or until the sauce has thickened and the shrimp are cooked through.

- Before serving, garnish the spicy shrimp stir fry with chopped green onions and sesame seeds.

- Serve the spicy shrimp stir fry over steamed rice and a salad of lettuce, carrots, cucumbers, and onions.

Nutritional Information (per serving):

Calories: 206

Protein: 26g

Fat: 8g

Carbohydrates: 9g

Fiber: 0g

Sodium: 574mg

Korean Spicy Scallop Stir Fry (Jeonbok Bokkeum)

Jeonbok bokkeum, also known as spicy scallop stir fry, is a famous Korean meal that consists of stir-fried scallops and veggies in a spicy and flavorful sauce. It's simple to prepare, tasty, and pairs great with steamed rice and a variety of vegetables.

Total Time: 30 minutes

Servings: 4

Ingredients:

1 lb large scallops

2 tbsp vegetable oil

2 cloves garlic, minced

1 tsp gochujang (Korean red pepper paste)

1 tsp soy sauce

1 tsp sugar

1/2 cup water

1 green onion, finely chopped

Sesame seeds, for garnish

Directions:

• In a large saucepan over medium heat, heat the vegetable oil. Stir in the minced garlic for 30 seconds, or until fragrant.

• Stir-fry the scallops in the pan for 2-3 minutes, or until they are cooked through.

• Combine the gochujang, soy sauce, sugar, and water in a mixing bowl. Bring the mixture to a boil, then lower to a low heat and continue to cook for 5-7 minutes, or until the sauce has thickened and the scallops are cooked through.

• Before serving, garnish the spicy scallop stir fry with chopped green onions and sesame seeds.

• Serve the spicy scallop stir fry over steamed rice and a salad of lettuce, carrots, cucumbers, and onions.

Nutritional Information (per serving):

Calories: 214

Protein: 27g

Fat: 8g

Carbohydrates: 9g

Fiber: 0g

Sodium: 574mg

Korean Spicy Pork (Daeji Bulgogi)

Daeji Bulgogi, or spicy pork, is a famous Korean meal prepared with thin slices of marinated pork that are perfectly grilled or pan-fried. It's delicious, salty, and somewhat sweet, and it works nicely with steaming rice and veggies.

Total Time: 30 minutes

Servings: 4

Ingredients:

1 lb thinly sliced pork (such as pork shoulder or pork belly)

1/4 cup gochujang (Korean red pepper paste)

2 tbsp soy sauce

2 tbsp brown sugar

1 tbsp sesame oil

2 cloves garlic, minced

1 green onion, finely chopped

1/2 tsp black pepper

1/2 tsp sesame seeds

Directions:

• Mix the gochujang, soy sauce, brown sugar, sesame oil, minced garlic, and chopped green onion, black pepper, and sesame seeds in a small bowl. To create the marinade, combine all of the ingredients in a mixing bowl.

• Pour the marinade over the pork pieces in a large mixing basin. Massage the marinade into the pork slices with your hands, ensuring that they are uniformly coated.

• Refrigerate the pork for at least 30 minutes, or up to 8 hours, after wrapping it in plastic wrap.

• Preheat a grill or a big skillet on high.

• Grill or pan-fry the pork slices in batches, being careful not to overcrowd the pan, for 2-3 minutes each side, or until done to your liking.

- Serve the spicy pork over steamed rice and a salad of lettuce, carrots, cucumbers, and onions.

Nutritional Information (per serving):

Calories: 307

Protein: 24g

Fat: 20g

Carbohydrates: 15g

Fiber: 0g

Sodium: 696mg

Korean Spicy Squid Stir Fry (Ojingeo Bokkeum)

Ojingeo bokkeum, also known as spicy squid stir fry, is a famous Korean meal that consists of stir-fried squid and veggies in a spicy and flavorful sauce. It's simple to prepare, tasty, and pairs great with steamed rice and a variety of vegetables.

Total Time: 30 minutes

Servings: 4

Ingredients:

1 lb squid, cleaned and cut into small pieces

2 tbsp vegetable oil

2 cloves garlic, minced

1 tsp gochujang (Korean red pepper paste)

1 tsp soy sauce

1 tsp sugar

1/2 cup water

1 green onion, finely chopped

Sesame seeds, for garnish

Directions:

- In a large saucepan over medium heat, heat the vegetable oil. Stir in the minced garlic for 30 seconds, or until fragrant.

- Stir-fry the squid in the pan for 2-3 minutes, or until it is cooked through.

- Combine the gochujang, soy sauce, sugar, and water in a mixing bowl.

- Bring the mixture to a boil, then lower to a low heat and cook for 5-7 minutes, or until the sauce has thickened and the squid is cooked through.

- Before serving, garnish the spicy squid stir fry with chopped green onions and sesame seeds.

- Serve the spicy squid stir fry over steaming rice and a salad of lettuce, carrots, cucumbers, and onions.

Nutritional Information (per serving):

Calories: 214

Protein: 26g

Fat: 8g

Carbohydrates: 9g

Fiber: 0g

Sodium: 574mg

Korean Spicy Crab Stir Fry (Jangeo Bokkeum)

Jangeo bokkeum, often known as spicy crab stir fry, is a famous Korean meal that consists of stir-fried crab and veggies in a spicy and flavorful sauce. It's simple to prepare, tasty, and pairs great with steamed rice and a variety of vegetables.

Total Time: 30 minutes

Servings: 4

Ingredients:

1 lb crab meat

2 tbsp vegetable oil

2 cloves garlic, minced

1 tsp gochujang (Korean red pepper paste)

1 tsp soy sauce

1 tsp sugar

1/2 cup water

1 green onion, finely chopped

Sesame seeds, for garnish

Directions:

- In a large saucepan over medium heat, heat the vegetable oil. Stir in the minced garlic for 30 seconds, or until fragrant.

- Stir-fry the crab flesh in the pan for 2-3 minutes, or until it is cooked through.

- Mix the gochujang, soy sauce, sugar, and water in a mixing bowl.

- Bring the mixture to a boil, then lower to a low heat and cook for 5-7 minutes, or until the sauce thickens and the crab is thoroughly cooked.

- Before serving, garnish the spicy crab stir fry with chopped green onions and sesame seeds.

- Serve the spicy crab stir fry over steamed rice and a salad of lettuce, carrots, cucumbers, and onions.

Nutritional Information (per serving):

Calories: 214

Protein: 26g

Fat: 8g

Carbohydrates: 9g

Fiber: 0g

Sodium: 574mg

Korean Spicy Clam Stir Fry (Jogae Bokkeum)

Jogae bokkeum, also known as spicy clam stir fry, is a famous Korean cuisine that consists of stir-fried clams and veggies in a spicy and flavorful sauce. It's simple to prepare, tasty, and pairs great with steamed rice and a variety of vegetables.

Total Time: 30 minutes

Servings: 4

Ingredients:

1 lb clams, cleaned

2 tbsp vegetable oil

2 cloves garlic, minced

1 tsp gochujang (Korean red pepper paste)

1 tsp soy sauce

1 tsp sugar

1/2 cup water

1 green onion, finely chopped

Sesame seeds, for garnish

Directions:

• In a large saucepan over medium heat, heat the vegetable oil. Stir in the minced garlic for 30 seconds, or until fragrant.

• Stir-fry the clams in the pan for 2-3 minutes, or until they are cooked through.

- Combine the gochujang, soy sauce, sugar, and water in a mixing bowl.

- Bring the mixture to a boil, then lower to a low heat and continue to cook for 5-7 minutes, or until the sauce has thickened and the clams are thoroughly cooked.

- Before serving, garnish the spicy clam stir fry with chopped green onions and sesame seeds.

- Serve the spicy clam stir fry over steamed rice and a salad of lettuce, carrots, cucumbers, and onions.

Nutritional Information (per serving):

Calories: 214

Protein: 26g

Fat: 8g

Carbohydrates: 9g

Fiber: 0g

Sodium: 574mg

Korean Spicy Chicken and Vegetable Stir Fry (Dak Bokkeum)

Dak bokkeum, also known as spicy chicken and vegetable stir fry, is a famous Korean cuisine that consists of stir-fried chicken and vegetables in a spicy and flavorful sauce. It's simple to prepare, tasty, and pairs great with steamed rice and a variety of vegetables.

Total Time: 30 minutes

Servings: 4

Ingredients:

1 lb boneless, skinless chicken breasts or thighs, cut into small pieces

2 tbsp vegetable oil

2 cloves garlic, minced

1 tsp gochujang (Korean red pepper paste)

1 tsp soy sauce

1 tsp sugar

1/2 cup water

1 green onion, finely chopped

Sesame seeds, for garnish

Assorted vegetables, such as carrots, bell peppers, onions, and mushrooms

Directions:

• In a large saucepan over medium heat, heat the vegetable oil. Stir in the minced garlic for 30 seconds, or until fragrant.

• Stir-fry the chicken pieces for 2-3 minutes, or until they are cooked through.

• Mix the gochujang, soy sauce, sugar, and water in a mixing bowl.

• Bring the mixture to a boil, then lower to a low heat and continue to cook for 5-7 minutes, or until the sauce has thickened and the chicken is cooked through.

• Transfer the veggies to the pan and stir-fry for another 2-3 minutes, or until they are cooked to your liking.

• Before serving, garnish the spicy chicken and vegetable stir fry with chopped green onions and sesame seeds.

- Serve the spicy chicken and vegetable stir fry with steaming rice and veggies like lettuce, carrots, cucumbers, and onions.

Nutritional Information (per serving):

Calories: 214

Protein: 26g

Fat: 8g

Carbohydrates: 9g

Fiber: 0g

Sodium: 574mg

Korean Spicy Beef and Vegetable Stir Fry (Bulgogi Bokkeum)

Bulgogi bokkeum, also known as spicy beef and vegetable stir fry, is a famous Korean cuisine that consists of stir-fried beef and vegetables in a spicy and flavorful sauce. It's simple to prepare, tasty, and pairs great with steamed rice and a variety of vegetables.

Total Time: 30 minutes

Servings: 4

Ingredients:

1 lb thinly sliced beef (such as sirloin, rib eye, or tenderloin)

2 tbsp vegetable oil

2 cloves garlic, minced

1 tsp gochujang (Korean red pepper paste)

1 tsp soy sauce

1 tsp sugar

1/2 cup water

1 green onion, finely chopped

Sesame seeds, for garnish

Assorted vegetables, such as carrots, bell peppers, onions, and mushrooms

Directions:

- In a large saucepan over medium heat, heat the vegetable oil. Stir in the minced garlic for 30 seconds, or until fragrant.

- Add the beef slices to the pan and heat for 2-3 minutes, or until they are cooked to your liking.

- Combine the gochujang, soy sauce, sugar, and water in a mixing bowl. Bring the mixture to a boil, then lower to a low heat and cook for 5-7 minutes, or until the sauce thickens and the meat is thoroughly cooked.

- Return the veggies to the pan and stir-fry for another 2-3 minutes, or until they are cooked to your liking.

- Before serving, garnish the spicy beef and vegetable stir fry with chopped green onions and sesame seeds.

- Serve the spicy beef and vegetable stir fry with steaming rice and veggies like lettuce, carrots, cucumbers, and onions.

Nutritional Information (per serving):

Calories: 214

Protein: 26g

Fat: 8g

Carb

Korean Multigrain Rice (Japgok-bap) with eggs and vegetables

Japgok-bap is a famous Korean meal cooked with a variety of grains, including brown rice, black rice, and millet, and topped with eggs and veggies. It is nutritious, flavorful, and complements a wide range of foods.

Total Time: 45 minutes

Servings: 4

Ingredients:

1 cup multigrain rice (such as brown rice, black rice, and millet)

2 cups water

4 eggs

2 tbsp vegetable oil

2 cloves garlic, minced

Assorted vegetables, such as carrots, bell peppers, onions, and mushrooms

2 tbsp soy sauce

1 tsp sesame oil

1 green onion, finely chopped

Sesame seeds, for garnish

Directions:

• In a fine mesh strainer, rinse the multigrain rice under cold water until the water runs clear.

• Bring the water to a boil in a medium saucepan over high heat.

• Return the washed multigrain rice to the pot and bring back to a boil. Reduce the heat to low, cover the pot, and cook the rice for 30-35 minutes, or until the water has been absorbed and the rice is thoroughly cooked.

• Meanwhile, melt the butter in a small pan over medium heat. Add the eggs to the skillet and heat until the whites are totally set and the yolks are done to your liking. Set aside the eggs.

• In a large saucepan over medium heat, heat the vegetable oil.

- Stir in the minced garlic for 30 seconds, or until fragrant.

- Add the veggies to the pan and stir-fry for 2-3 minutes, or until they're cooked to your liking.

- Stir in the soy sauce and sesame oil until fully combined.

- When the multigrain rice is done, divide it equally between four bowls.

- Arrange the stir-fried veggies, a cooked egg, and chopped green onions on top of each dish of rice.

- Before serving, sprinkle with sesame seeds.

Nutritional Information (per serving):

Calories: 348

Protein: 11g

Fat: 15g

Carbohydrates: 46g

Fiber: 4g

Sodium: 672mg

Korean Fried Chicken (Dakgangjeong) with steamed rice and vegetables

Dakgangjeong is a famous Korean meal that consists of deep-fried chicken covered in a sweet and spicy sauce. It's tasty and crispy, and it combines great with steaming rice and a variety of veggies.

Total Time: 45 minutes

Servings: 4

Ingredients:

1 lb chicken wings or drumettes

1 cup all-purpose flour

1 tsp salt

1 tsp black pepper

1 cup water

1 cup cornstarch

Vegetable oil, for frying

2 cloves garlic, minced

2 tbsp gochujang (Korean red pepper paste)

2 tbsp honey

2 tbsp soy sauce

1 tsp vinegar

1 green onion, finely chopped

Sesame seeds, for garnish

Directions:

- In a medium mixing bowl, combine the flour, salt, and black pepper. Stir in the water until a smooth batter forms.
- In a small bowl, combine the cornstarch and water. Each chicken wing or drumette should be dipped in the batter and then coated with cornstarch.
- In a big saucepan or deep fryer, heat the vegetable oil over medium heat until it reaches 375°F.
- Fry the battered and coated chicken pieces in the heated oil for 8-10 minutes, or until golden brown and cooked through.
- Make the sauce while the chicken is cooking. Combine the minced garlic, gochujang, honey, soy sauce, and vinegar in a small pot.
- Cook, stirring often, over medium heat until the sauce comes to a boil.

- When the chicken is done, remove it from the oil and drain it on a platter lined with paper towels.
- Melt the butter in a large saucepan over medium heat. Toss the fried chicken in the pan until it is uniformly covered in the sauce.
- Before serving, garnish the Korean fried chicken with chopped green onions and sesame seeds.
- Serve with steamed rice and a variety of vegetables, such as lettuce, carrots, cucumbers, and onions.

Nutritional Information (per serving):

Calories: 483

Protein: 27g

Fat: 27g

Carbohydrates: 37g

Fiber: 1g

Sodium: 1224mg

Korean Rice Balls (Onigiri) filled with vegetables and pickled plum

Onigiri, or rice balls, are a popular snack in Korea and Japan. They are prepared from rice that has been molded into a triangular or cylindrical form and filled with a variety of ingredients such as vegetables and pickled plum. They're simple to prepare, portable, and make an excellent snack or lunch option.

Total Time: 45 minutes

Servings: 4

Ingredients:

2 cups short grain rice

2 1/2 cups water

1 tsp salt

Assorted vegetables, such as carrots, bell peppers, onions, and mushrooms

4 pickled plums (umeboshi)

4 sheets of nori seaweed

Directions:

• In a fine mesh strainer, rinse the short grain rice under cold water until the water runs clear.

• Bring the water to a boil in a medium saucepan over high heat. Return the washed short grain rice and salt to the pot and heat to a boil.

• Reduce the heat to low, cover the pot, and cook the rice for 20-25 minutes, or until the water has been absorbed and the rice is thoroughly cooked.

• In the meanwhile, finely chop the veggies and put aside.

• Transfer the rice to a large mixing bowl after it has finished cooking. Gently stir the rice with a rice paddle or a wooden spoon until it gets somewhat sticky.

• Form a handful of rice into a triangular or cylindrical form.

• In the center of the rice, press a pickled plum and a small handful of chopped veggies.

• Gently wrap a strip of nori seaweed around the rice ball to hold the stuffing within.

- Continue with the remaining rice, fillings, and nori seaweed.

- Serve the Korean rice balls as a snack or as a lunch alternative; they may be eaten right away or covered in plastic wrap and refrigerated for later.

Nutritional Information (per serving):

Calories: 280

Protein: 5g

Fat: 1g

Carbohydrates: 63g

Fiber: 2g

Sodium: 456mg

Korean-style Pancakes (Jeons) filled with Vegetables and seafood

Jeons, or Korean-style pancakes, are a popular Korean meal created with a variety of contents, including vegetables and seafood, combined into a pancake batter and baked in a skillet until crispy and golden brown.

They're simple to prepare, tasty, and go great with a variety of dipping sauces.

Total Time: 30 minutes

Servings: 4

Ingredients:

1 cup all-purpose flour

1 cup water

2 eggs

1 tsp salt

2 tbsp vegetable oil, plus more for frying

Assorted vegetables, such as carrots, bell peppers, onions, and mushrooms

1 cup seafood, such as shrimp or squid, finely chopped

Green onions, finely chopped, for garnish

Directions:

- In a medium mixing bowl, combine the flour, water, eggs, and salt to make a smooth batter.

- In a large saucepan over medium heat, heat the vegetable oil.

Mix in the veggies and shellfish with the pancake batter until fully combined.

- Drop spoonfuls of the pancake batter onto the heated pan, making tiny to medium-sized pancakes.
- Cook for 2-3 minutes on each side, or until the pancakes are crispy and golden brown.
- Remove the pancakes from the pan and drain them on a platter lined with paper towels.
- Continue with the remaining pancake batter until all of the pan-cakes are cooked.
- Before serving, garnish the Korean-style pancakes with chopped green onions.
- Serve the Korean-style pancakes with dipping sauces such soy sauce, vinegar, or gochujang.

Nutritional Information (per serving):

Calories: 199

Protein: 9g

Fat: 9g

Carbohydrates: 21g

Fiber: 1g

Sodium: 615mg

Korean Multigrain Rice (Japgokbap) with eggs and vegetables

Japgokbap is a famous Korean meal cooked with a variety of grains, including brown rice, black rice, and millet, and topped with eggs and veggies. It is nutritious, flavorful, and complements a wide range of foods.

Total Time: 45 minutes

Servings: 4

Ingredients:

1 cup multigrain rice (such as brown rice, black rice, and millet)

2 cups water

4 eggs

2 tbsp vegetable oil

2 cloves garlic, minced

Assorted vegetables, such as carrots, bell peppers, onions, and mushrooms

2 tbsp soy sauce

1 tsp sesame oil

1 green onion, finely chopped

Sesame seeds, for garnish

Directions:

- In a fine mesh strainer, rinse the multigrain rice under cold water until the water runs clear.

- Bring the water to a boil in a medium saucepan over high heat. Return the washed multigrain rice to the pot and heat to a boil.

- Reduce the heat to low, cover the pot, and cook the rice for 30-35 minutes, or until the water has been absorbed and the rice is thoroughly cooked.

- Meanwhile, melt the butter in a small pan over medium heat. Add the eggs to the skillet and heat until the whites are totally set and the yolks are done to your liking. Set aside the eggs.

- In a large saucepan over medium heat, heat the vegetable oil. Stir in the minced garlic for 30 seconds, or until fragrant.

- Add the veggies to the pan and stir-fry for 2-3 minutes, or until they're cooked to your liking.

- Stir in the soy sauce and sesame oil until fully combined.

- When the multigrain rice is done, divide it equally between four bowls.

- Before serving, top each bowl of rice with the stir-fried veggies, a cooked egg, and chopped green onions, and garnish with sesame seeds.

Nutritional Information (per serving):

Calories: 348

Protein: 11g

Fat: 15g

Carbohydrates: 46g

Fiber: 4g

Sodium: 672mg

Korean Soft Tofu Stew (Soondubu Jjigae)

Soondubu jjigae is a traditional Korean stew prepared with soft tofu, veggies, and a range of meats including beef or fish. It's filling, savory, and goes nicely with steaming rice.

Total Time: 30 minutes

Servings: 4

Ingredients:

4 cups water

4 anchovy packets or 1 cup anchovy broth

2 cloves garlic, minced

1 tsp gochugaru (Korean red pepper flakes)

1 tsp soy sauce

1 tsp salt

1 tsp sugar

1 package soft tofu, cut into small cubes

Assorted vegetables, such as zucchini, bell peppers, onions, and mushrooms

4 oz beef, thinly sliced

2 green onions, finely chopped

Sesame seeds, for garnish

Directions:

• Bring the water, anchovy packets or broth, minced garlic, go-chugaru, soy sauce, salt, and sugar to a boil in a large saucepan over high heat.

• Stir in the tofu, veggies, and meat until completely combined.

• Simmer the stew for 10-15 minutes, or until the vegetables are soft and the meat is cooked through.

• Before serving, garnish the stew with chopped green onions and sesame seeds.

• Serve the Korean soft tofu stew over steaming rice.

Nutritional Information (per serving):

Calories: 182

Protein: 14g

Fat: 9g

Carbohydrates: 14g

Fiber: 2g

Sodium: 870mg

Korean Spicy Beef Soup (Yukgaejang)

Yukgaejang is a traditional Korean soup comprised of thinly sliced beef, veggies, and seasonings. It's spicy and delicious, and it pairs nicely with steamed rice.

Total Time: 1 hour

Servings: 4

Ingredients:

4 cups water

4 anchovy packets or 1 cup anchovy broth

2 cloves garlic, minced

1 tsp gochugaru (Korean red pepper flakes)

1 tsp soy sauce

1 tsp salt

1 tsp sugar

1 lb beef, thinly sliced

Assorted vegetables, such as zucchini, bell peppers, onions, and mushrooms

4 green onions, finely chopped

Sesame seeds, for garnish

Directions:

• Bring the water, anchovy packets or broth, minced garlic, go-chugaru, soy sauce, salt, and sugar to a boil in a large saucepan over high heat.

• Add the meat and veggies to the saucepan and mix thoroughly.

• Simmer the soup for 45 minutes to an hour, or until the meat is soft and the veggies are thoroughly cooked.

• Before serving, garnish the soup with chopped green onions and sesame seeds.

• Serve the Korean spicy beef soup over steaming rice.

Nutritional Information (per serving):

Calories: 213

Protein: 26g

Fat: 8g

Carbohydrates: 15g

Fiber: 2g

Sodium: 946mg

Korean Seaweed Soup (Miyeokguk)

Miyeokguk (seaweed, beef, and veggies) is a popular Korean soup. It's filling, savory, and pairs nicely with steaming rice.

Total Time: 45 minutes

Servings: 4

Ingredients:

4 cups water

4 anchovy packets or 1 cup anchovy broth

1 cup dried seaweed (miyeok)

1 lb beef, thinly sliced

Assorted vegetables, such as zucchini, bell peppers, onions, and mushrooms

2 green onions, finely chopped

Sesame seeds, for garnish

Directions

• Bring the water and anchovy packets or broth to a boil in a large saucepan over high heat.

• Cook for 5 minutes after adding the dried seaweed to the saucepan.

• Add the meat and veggies to the saucepan and mix thoroughly.

• Reduce the heat to low and continue to cook the soup for 30-35 minutes, or until the meat is soft and the veggies are tender.

• Before serving, garnish the soup with chopped green onions and sesame seeds.

• Serve the Korean seaweed soup with steaming rice.

Nutritional Information (per serving):

Calories: 200

Protein: 26g

Fat: 8g

Korean Chicken Soup (Dakgaejang)

Dakgaejang (Chicken, Vegetables, and Spices) is a popular Korean soup. It's flavorful and filling, and it works nicely with steamed rice.

Total Time: 45 minutes

Servings: 4

Ingredients:

4 cups water

4 anchovy packets or 1 cup anchovy broth

2 cloves garlic, minced

1 tsp gochugaru (Korean red pepper flakes)

1 tsp soy sauce

1 tsp salt

1 tsp sugar

1 lb chicken, thinly sliced

Assorted vegetables, such as zucchini, bell peppers, onions, and mushrooms

4 green onions, finely chopped

Sesame seeds, for garnish

Directions:

• Bring the water, anchovy packets or broth, minced garlic, go-chugaru, soy sauce, salt, and sugar to a boil in a large saucepan over high heat.

• Add the chicken and veggies to the pot and mix thoroughly.

• Reduce the heat to low and stew the soup for 30-35 minutes, or until the chicken is thoroughly cooked and the vegetables are tender.

• Before serving, garnish the soup with chopped green onions and sesame seeds.

• Serve the Korean chicken soup over steaming rice.

Nutritional Information (per serving):

Calories: 176

Protein: 23g

Fat: 7g

Carbohydrates: 14g

Fiber: 2g

Sodium: 834mg

Korean Mushroom Soup (Beoseot Gomtang)

Beoseot gomtang, or mushroom and beef broth soup, is a popular Korean dish. It's flavorful and filling, and it works nicely with steamed rice.

Total Time: 45 minutes

Servings: 4

Ingredients:

4 cups beef broth

1 lb mushrooms, thinly sliced

1 lb beef, thinly sliced

2 green onions, finely chopped

Sesame seeds, for garnish

Directions:

- Bring the beef broth to a boil in a large saucepan over high heat.

- Add the mushrooms and meat to the saucepan and mix thoroughly. Reduce the heat to low and continue to cook the soup for 30-35

Minutes, or until the meat is tender and the mushrooms are tender.

- Before serving, garnish the soup with chopped green onions and sesame seeds.

- Serve the Korean mushroom soup over steaming rice.

Nutritional Information (per serving):

Calories: 246

Protein: 24g

Fat: 12g

Carbohydrates: 16g

Fiber: 3g

Sodium: 678mg

Korean Ox Tail Soup (Kkorijjim)

Kkorijjim is a traditional Korean soup composed of ox tail, veggies, and spices. It's flavorful and filling, and it works nicely with steamed rice.

Total Time: 2 hours

Servings: 4

Ingredients:

4 cups water

4 anchovy packets or 1 cup anchovy broth

2 cloves garlic, minced

1 tsp gochugaru (Korean red pepper flakes)

1 tsp soy sauce

1 tsp salt

1 tsp sugar

1 lb ox tail, cut into small pieces

Assorted vegetables, such as zucchini, bell peppers, onions, and mushrooms

4 green onions, finely chopped

Sesame seeds, for garnish

Directions:

• Bring the water and anchovy packets or broth to a boil in a large saucepan over high heat.

• To the saucepan, put the ox tail, minced garlic, go-chugaru, soy sauce, salt, and sugar.

• Reduce the heat to low and continue to cook the soup for 1-1.5 hours, or until the ox tail is soft and the flavors have combined.

•Cook for a further 15-20 minutes, or until the veggies are thoroughly cooked, after adding the vegetables to the saucepan.

• Before serving, garnish the soup with chopped green onions and sesame seeds.

• Serve the Korean ox tail soup over steaming rice.

Nutritional Information (per serving):

Calories: 295

Protein: 26g

Fat: 16g

Carbohydrates: 16g

Fiber: 2g

Sodium: 925mg

Korean Pork Belly Soup (Samgyetang)

Samgyetang is a famous Korean soup that is prepared with a whole young chicken that has been filled with rice, ginseng, and other medicinal herbs. It's filling, savory, and goes nicely with steaming rice.

Total Time: 2 hours

Servings: 4

Ingredients:

4 cups water

4 anchovy packets or 1 cup anchovy broth

1 whole young chicken, about 1.5 lbs

1/4 cup glutinous rice

2 cloves garlic, minced

1 piece of dried ginseng, about the size of your thumb

1 tsp salt

1 tsp black pepper

4 green onions, finely chopped

Sesame seeds, for garnish

Directions:

• Bring the water and anchovy packets or broth to a boil in a large saucepan over high heat.

• Rinse and pat dry the chicken with paper towels.

• Combine the glutinous rice, minced garlic, and a touch of salt in a small bowl. Stuff the mixture into the chicken's cavity. Combine the chicken, ginseng, salt, and black pepper in a saucepan.

- Reduce the heat to low and continue to cook the soup for 1-1.5 hours, or until the chick-en is soft and the rice is tender.
- Before serving, garnish the soup with chopped green onions and sesame seeds.
- Serve the Korean pork belly soup over steaming rice.

Nutritional Information (per serving):

Calories: 350

Protein: 37g

Fat: 17g

Carbohydrates: 22g

Fiber: 2g

Sodium: 828mg

Korean Spicy Oyster Soup (Gul Jjigae)

Gul jjigae is a traditional Korean soup comprised of oysters, veggies, and spices. It's spicy and flavorful, and it works great with steamed rice.

Total Time: 45 minutes

Servings: 4

Ingredients:

4 cups water

4 anchovy packets or 1 cup anchovy broth

2 cloves garlic, minced

1 tsp gochugaru (Korean red pepper flakes)

1 tsp soy sauce

1 tsp salt

1 tsp sugar

1 lb oysters

Assorted vegetables, such as zucchini, bell peppers, onions, and mushrooms

4 green onions, finely chopped

Sesame seeds, for garnish

Directions:

- Bring the water, anchovy packets or broth, minced garlic, go-chugaru, soy sauce, salt, and sugar to a boil in a large saucepan over high heat.

- Add the oysters and veggies to the saucepan and mix thoroughly.

- Simmer the soup for 20-25 minutes, or until the oysters are thoroughly cooked and the vegetables are soft.

- Before serving, garnish the soup with chopped green onions and sesame seeds.

- Serve the hot Korean oyster soup with steaming rice.

Nutritional Information (per serving):

Calories: 191

Protein: 21g

Fat: 7g

Carbohydrates: 16g

Fiber: 2g

Sodium: 892mg

Korean Mushroom Soup (Beoseot Gomtang)

Beoseot gomtang, or mushroom and beef broth soup, is a popular Korean dish. It's flavorful and filling, and it works nicely with steamed rice.

Total Time: 45 minutes

Servings: 4

Ingredients:

4 cups beef broth

1 lb mushrooms, thinly sliced

1 lb beef, thinly sliced

2 green onions, finely chopped

Sesame seeds, for garnish

Directions:

- Bring the beef broth to a boil in a large saucepan over high heat.

- Add the mushrooms and meat to the saucepan and mix thoroughly.

- Lower the heat to low and continue to cook the soup for 30-35 minutes, or until the meat is soft and the mushrooms are thoroughly cooked.
- Before serving, garnish the soup with chopped green onions and sesame seeds.
- Serve the Korean mushroom soup over steaming rice.

Nutritional Information (per serving):

Calories: 246

Protein: 24g

Fat: 12g

Carbohydrates: 16g

Fiber: 3g

Sodium: 678mg

Korean Seaweed Soup (Miyeokguk)

Miyeokguk (seaweed and beef broth) is a popular Korean soup. It's filling, savory, and goes nicely with steaming rice.

Total Time: 45 minutes

Servings: 4

Ingredients:

4 cups beef broth

1/2 cup dried seaweed, soaked in water for 30 minutes and then drained

1/2 lb beef, thinly sliced

2 green onions, finely chopped

Sesame seeds, for garnish

Directions:

- Bring the beef broth to a boil in a large saucepan over high heat.

- Add the seaweed and meat to the saucepan and mix thoroughly.

- Reduce the heat to low and stew the soup for 20-25 minutes, or until the meat is soft and the seaweed is cooked through.

- Before serving, garnish the soup with chopped green onions and sesame seeds.

- Serve the Korean seaweed soup with steaming rice.

Nutritional Information (per serving):

Calories: 173

Protein: 20g

Fat: 7g

Carbohydrates: 14g

Fiber: 3g

Sodium: 678mg

Korean Beef and Radish Soup (Moo Saengchae)

A popular Korean soup prepared with beef, radish, and spices called Moo Saengchae. It's flavorful and nutritious, and it works nicely with steamed rice.

Total Time: 45 minutes

Servings: 4

Ingredients:

4 cups water

4 anchovy packets or 1 cup anchovy broth

1/2 lb beef, thinly sliced

1 large radish, peeled and cut into thin slices

2 cloves garlic, minced

1 tsp gochugaru (Korean red pepper flakes)

1 tsp soy sauce

1 tsp salt

1 tsp sugar

2 green onions, finely chopped

Sesame seeds, for garnish

Directions:

- Bring the water and anchovy packets or broth to a boil in a large saucepan over high heat.

- To the saucepan, put the meat, radish, minced garlic, go-chugaru, soy sauce, salt, and sugar.

- Reduce the heat to low and stew the soup for 20-25 minutes, or until the meat is soft and the radish is cooked through.
- Before serving, garnish the soup with chopped green onions and sesame seeds.
- Serve the Korean beef and radish soup over steaming rice.

Nutritional Information (per serving):

Calories: 187

Protein: 20g

Fat: 7g

Carbohydrates: 16g

Fiber: 2g

Sodium: 757mg

Korean Sweet Rice Balls (Gyeongdan)

Gyeongdan is a famous Korean delicacy made from sticky rice flour and filled with sweet bean paste. It's sweet and chewy, and it pairs nicely with a cup of tea.Total Time: 45 minutes

Servings: 15-20 balls

Ingredients:

1 cup glutinous rice flour

1/2 cup water

1/2 cup sweet bean filling (such as red bean or black sesame)

Directions:

• In a medium mixing basin, combine the glutinous rice flour and water to make a smooth dough.

• Cut the dough into 15-20 even pieces.

• Flatten one piece of dough in the palm of your hand. Fill the middle of the dough with a tablespoon of sweet bean filling.

• Pinch the dough's edges together to seal the filling within. Set aside the dough after rolling it into a ball.

• Repeat with the rest of the dough and filling.

• Over high heat, bring a saucepan of water to a boil.

- Gently place the rice balls in the boiling water and cook for 10-15 minutes, or until they float to the surface.

- With a slotted spoon, remove the rice balls from the saucepan and drain any extra water.

- Serve the Korean sweet rice balls at room temperature or warm.

Nutritional Information (per serving):

Calories: 69

Protein: 1g

Fat: 0g

Carbohydrates: 15g

Fiber: 1g

Sodium: 5mg

Korean Rice Cakes (Hwajeon) with sweet bean filling

Hwajeon is a classic Korean dish made from sticky rice flour and filled with sweet bean paste. It's sweet and chewy, and it pairs nicely with a cup of tea.

Total Time: 45 minutes

Servings: 15-20 cakes

Ingredients:

1 cup glutinous rice flour

1/2 cup water

1/2 cup sweet bean filling (such as red bean or black sesame)

1 tsp vegetable oil

Directions:

- In a medium mixing basin, combine the glutinous rice flour and water to make a smooth dough.

- Cut the dough into 15-20 even pieces.

- Flatten one piece of dough in the palm of your hand.

- Fill the middle of the dough with a tablespoon of sweet bean filling.

- Pinch the dough's edges together to seal the filling within.

- Set aside the dough after flattening it into a cake form. Rep with the rest of the dough and filling.

- Heat the vegetable oil in a large skillet over medium heat.

- Cook the rice cakes in the pan for 2-3 minutes on each side, or until gently browned.

- Warm or at room temperature, serve the Korean rice cakes.

Nutritional Information (per serving):

Calories: 69

Protein: 1g

Fat: 0g

Carbohydrates: 15g

Fiber: 1g

Sodium: 5mg

Korean Steamed Egg (Gyeran Jjim)

Gyeran jjim (steamed eggs and veggies) is a popular Korean egg dish. It's light and fluffy, and it works beautifully with steaming rice.

Total Time: 45 minutes

Servings: 4

Ingredients:

6 large eggs

1/2 cup water

1/2 cup milk

1/2 tsp salt

2 green onions, finely chopped

1/2 cup cooked vegetables, such as carrots, peas, and corn

Sesame seeds, for garnish

Directions:

- Break the eggs into a medium mixing basin and gently beat with a fork.

- Combine the eggs, water, milk, and salt in a mixing bowl.

- Fill a big steaming dish or a heat-resistant bowl halfway with the egg mixture.

- Place the steaming plate or bowl in the steamer and steam the eggs for 15-20 minutes, or until thoroughly cooked and set.

- Before serving, garnish the steaming eggs with chopped green onions and sesame seeds.

- Serve the steamed Korean eggs with a dish of steamed rice.

Nutritional Information (per serving):

Calories: 124

Protein: 10g

Fat: 7g

Carbohydrates: 6g

Fiber: 1g

Sodium: 361mg

Korean Glutinous Rice Cake (Tteokbokki)

Tteokbokki is a popular Korean snack made with glutinous rice cakes and spicy sauce. It is spicy, chewy, and goes well with a bowl of steamed rice.

Total Time: 45 minutes

Servings: 4

Ingredients:

8 oz glutinous rice cakes

1 cup water

1/2 cup gochujang (Korean red pepper paste)

1/2 cup soy sauce

1/2 cup sugar

2 green onions, finely chopped

2 cloves garlic, minced

1 tsp sesame oil

Vegetables, such as onions, bell peppers, and carrots (optional)

Directions:

- Soak the glutinous rice cakes for 15-20 minutes in cold water, or until soft.

- Bring the water, gochujang, soy sauce, and sugar to a boil in a large saucepan over high heat.

- Stir in the soaked rice cakes, green onions, minced garlic, and sesame oil to mix.

- Reduce the heat to medium and cook the tteokbokki for 20-25 minutes, or until the sauce thickens and the rice cakes are cooked through.

- Add veggies such as onions, bell peppers, and carrots to the pan during the final 5 minutes of cooking if preferred.

- Serve the hot Korean glutinous rice cake (tteokbokki) with steamed rice.

Nutritional Information (per serving):

Calories: 358

Protein: 5g

Fat: 1g

Carbohydrates: 82g

Fiber: 1g

Sodium: 1680mg

Sweet and Sour Chicken (Tongdak)

Tongdak is a traditional Korean chicken dish with a sweet and sour sauce. It's flavorful and tender, and it works great with steaming rice.

Total Time: 45 minutes

Servings: 4

Ingredients:

1 lb chicken, cut into bite-sized pieces

1 cup water

1/2 cup vinegar

1/2 cup sugar

1/2 cup ketchup

2 cloves garlic, minced

1 tsp salt

1 tsp gochugaru (Korean red pepper flakes)

1 tsp cornstarch

Vegetables, such as onions, bell peppers, and carrots (optional)

Directions:

- Bring the water, vinegar, sugar, ketchup, minced garlic, salt, and gochugaru to a boil in a large saucepan over high heat.

- Add the chicken to the pan and coat well with the sauce.

- Lower the heat to medium and cook the chicken for 20-25 minutes, or until thoroughly cooked and tender.

- In a small mixing bowl, combine the cornstarch and 1 tablespoon of water to make a smooth paste.

- To thicken the sauce, add the cornstarch paste to the pan and stir thoroughly.

- Add veggies such as onions, bell peppers, and carrots to the pan during the final 5 minutes of cooking if preferred.

Nutritional Information (per serving):

Calories: 303

Protein: 23g

Fat: 6g

Carbohydrates: 42g

Fiber: 2g

Sodium: 988mg

Korean Red Bean Porridge (Danpatjuk)

Danpatjuk is a traditional Korean dessert comprised of red beans and rice. It's sweet and creamy, and it pairs beautifully with a cup of tea.

Total Time: 45 minutes

Servings: 4

Ingredients:

1 cup red beans, soaked overnight and drained

4 cups water

1/2 cup short-grain rice

1/2 cup sugar

1/2 tsp salt

2 green onions, finely chopped

Sesame seeds, for garnish

Directions:

• Bring the red beans and water to a boil in a large saucepan over high heat.

• Reduce the heat to low and continue to boil the beans for 1 hour, or until thoroughly cooked and soft.

• Stir in the rice, sugar, and salt until completely combined.

• Turn up the heat and bring the mixture to a boil.

• Lower the heat to low and continue to cook the porridge for 20-25 minutes, or until the rice is tender and the porridge has thickened.

• Before serving, garnish the cereal with chopped green onions and sesame seeds.

• Serve the Korean red bean porridge at room temperature or heated.

Nutritional Information (per serving):

Calories: 280

Protein: 10g

Fat: 1g

Carbohydrates: 62g

Fiber: 7g

Sodium: 163mg

Chapter 10:
Tips for adapting traditional Korean recipes to be gluten-free

Gluten-free diets have grown in popularity in recent years as individuals learn about the advantages of removing gluten from their diet. If you are gluten-free and appreciate traditional Korean cuisine, you may be wondering how to adjust these foods to satisfy your dietary requirements. Here are some gluten-free suggestions for traditional Korean recipes:

Use gluten-free flours: Wheat flour, which includes gluten, is often used in Korean cuisine. Alternative flours such as rice flour, potato starch, or almond flour may be used to make these recipes gluten-free. These flours are commonly accessible and may be used in most recipes as a 1:1 substitution for wheat flour.

Choose gluten-free condiments and sauces: Sauces and condiments are frequently used in Korean cuisine to give flavor and depth to meals. Gluten is present in certain popular Korean condiments and sauces, including soy sauce, hoisin sauce, and oyster sauce. Gluten-free substitutes like as tamari, coconut aminos, and gluten-free hoisin sauce may be used to make these dishes gluten-free.

Keep thickeners in mind: Some Korean recipes call for thickeners like wheat flour or cornstarch to give foods a creamy or thick texture. Gluten-free thickeners such as potato starch or arrowroot powder may be used to make these recipes gluten-free.

Use gluten-free noodles: Noodles manufactured from wheat flour, which contains gluten, are often used in Korean dishes. You may make these dishes gluten-free by using rice, potato, or bean flour noodles. Gluten-free noodles are widely available in supermarkets, or you may prepare your own using a gluten-free flour combination.

Prepare your own marinades: Because many pre-packaged marinades include gluten, it's recommended to make your own marinades using gluten-free ingredients. To make a tasty marinade for your Korean foods, combine gluten-free soy sauce, rice vinegar, sesame oil, and other gluten-free ingredients.

By following these guidelines, you may effortlessly convert traditional Korean recipes to be gluten-free and enjoy all of your favorite tastes and textures without sacrificing your dietary demands.

Recommendations for Gluten-free Korean Ingredients and products

If you're on a gluten-free diet and want to include more Korean tastes into your meals, you need be aware of the gluten-containing components and products. Gluten is often present in many Korean recipes and sauces and may be found in wheat, barley, and rye. Here are some gluten-free Korean ingredients and items to consider using in your cooking:

Rice & Noodles: Rice, sweet potato, and mung bean noodles are all naturally gluten-free choices that may be used as a basis for many Korean meals. Look for "gluten-free" labels to confirm that they were not contaminated with gluten during the production process.

Kimchi: Kimchi is a mainstay in Korean cuisine, and wheat flour is used as a thickening in many traditional recipes. However, gluten-free kimchi is widely available in Korean shops and online. Instead of wheat flour, look for kimchi prepared with rice flour or arrowroot starch.

Soy Sauce: Although soy sauce is a frequent component in many Korean cuisine, it is important to choose a gluten-free kind. Tamari soy sauce, which is produced entirely of soybeans, is a fantastic choice. Gluten-free soy sauces produced from rice or other alternative grains are also available.

Gochujang is a fiery and delicious Korean red pepper paste that is often used as a condiment or an ingredient in sauces and marinades. It's normally prepared using wheat flour, although gluten-free variants made with rice flour or other alternative grains are available.

Snacks and Sweets: Many Korean snacks and desserts include wheat flour or other gluten-containing ingredients. However, there are still lots of naturally gluten-free products available. Rice cakes, mochi, and sweet rice balls are all excellent choices, as are fruits and nuts.

You may enjoy the tastes of Korean cuisine while adhering to a gluten-free diet by using gluten-free foods and products. Read labels carefully and search for goods labeled "gluten-free" to guarantee you're obtaining the safest and most genuine items available.

Chapter 11:
Conclusion

In Conclusion, adhering to a gluten-free diet does not have to mean foregoing the flavors and traditions of Korean food. With the correct materials and tools, you can easily prepare tasty and fulfilling Korean meals at home that are gluten-free. Read labels carefully and search for goods labeled "gluten-free" to guarantee you're obtaining the safest and most genuine items available.

Rice and noodles, kimchi, soy sauce, gochujang, meats and seafood, vegetables, oils and fats, and spices and seasonings are all naturally gluten-free ingredients and items that may be used in Korean cuisine. You may still enjoy the tastes of Korean cuisine while adhering to a gluten-free diet by using these products and being careful of any marinades or spice mixes that may contain gluten.

With a little forethought and creativity, you can easily prepare a range of tasty and enjoyable gluten-free Korean meals that are acceptable

for all members of your family or group. Whether you like spicy stews, savory stir-fries, or sweet and tangy sauces, a gluten-free Korean cookbook has lots of alternatives. So don't be scared to try new recipes and explore - you could just find a new favorite meal!

Printed in Dunstable, United Kingdom